Suggested Registration:
Sw. 8. 4. 2. Mixtures
Gt. to 15th
Ch. 8. 4. 2. (+ mix.)
Ped. 16. 8. 4.
Sw. to Gt.
Sw. to Ch.
Sw. to Ped.
Gt. to Ped.

# TOCCATA

GEORGI MUSHEL

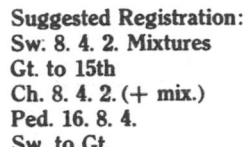

Allegro (♩ = 168)
MANUAL
PEDAL
Gt. *f*
2nd time add Gt. mixtures
Gt. 8. 4. 2.

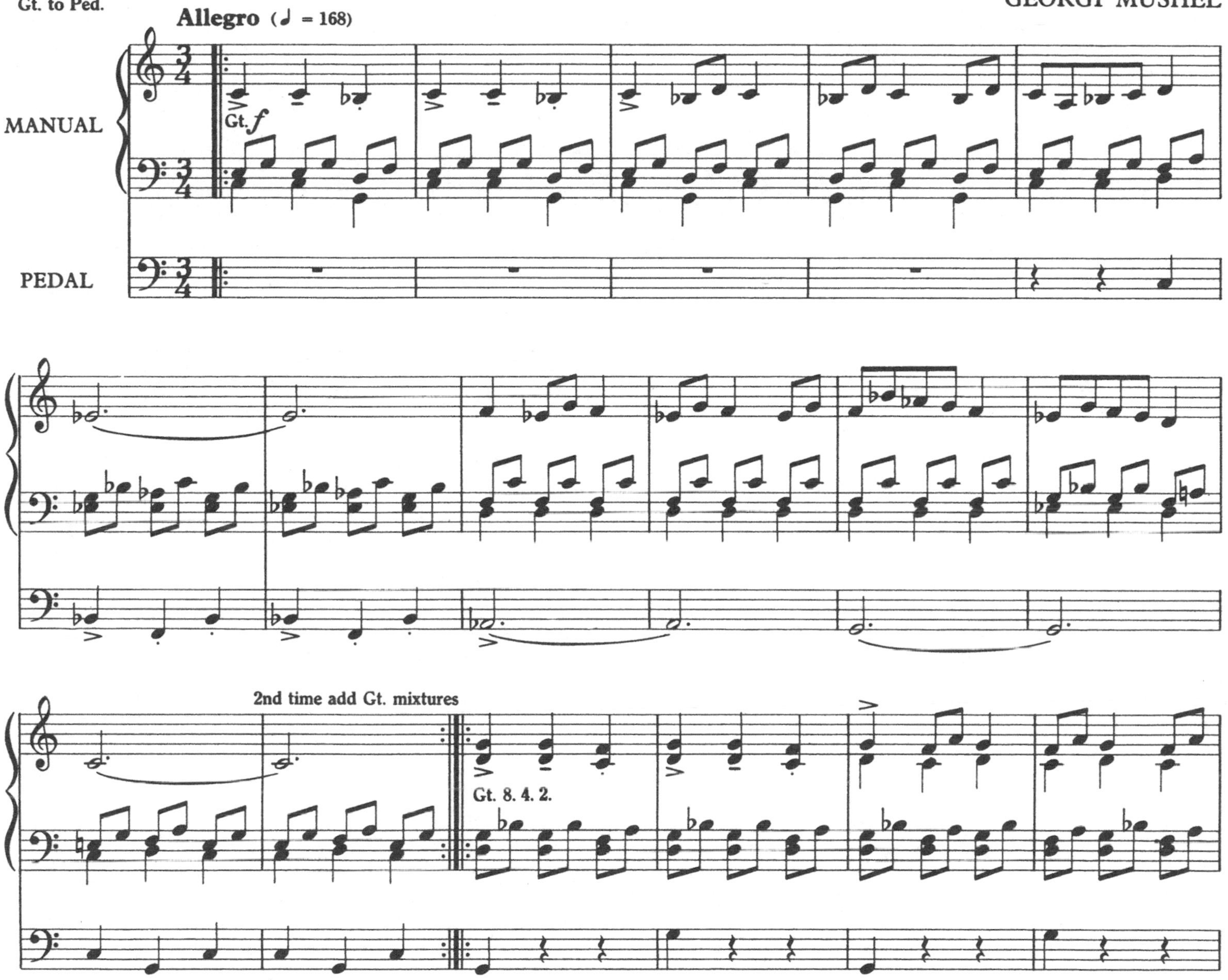

Duration 4½ minutes

The suggested registration is by Noel Rawsthorne who has recorded the piece on Ryemuse RP 7013 and ALR 1204.



Printed in Great Britain

OXFORD UNIVERSITY PRESS, MUSIC DEPARTMENT, GREAT CLARENDON STREET, OXFORD OX2 6DP

add Full Swell (box closed)

allargando

**a tempo**
add Gt. reeds

*poco stringendo*

**allargando**

# 9. Jazzy Jingle bells

J. Pierpont

Nos. 8 and 9 are reversed to avoid a page turn.

# 8. O leave your sheep

French folk tune

# 10. Allegretto in G

Mozart

# 11. The Mallow fling

Irish folk tune

# 12. Noël

Daquin

# 13. Finale from the 'Water Music'

Handel

# 14. Ecossaise in G

Beethoven

# 15. Fiddle Time rag

KB & DB

# 16. Busy day

KB & DB

# 17. On the go!

KB & DB

* The repeat is written out in full in the violin part.

# 19. Takin' it easy

KB & DB

* The repeat is written out in full in the violin part.
Nos. 18 and 19 are reversed to avoid a page turn.

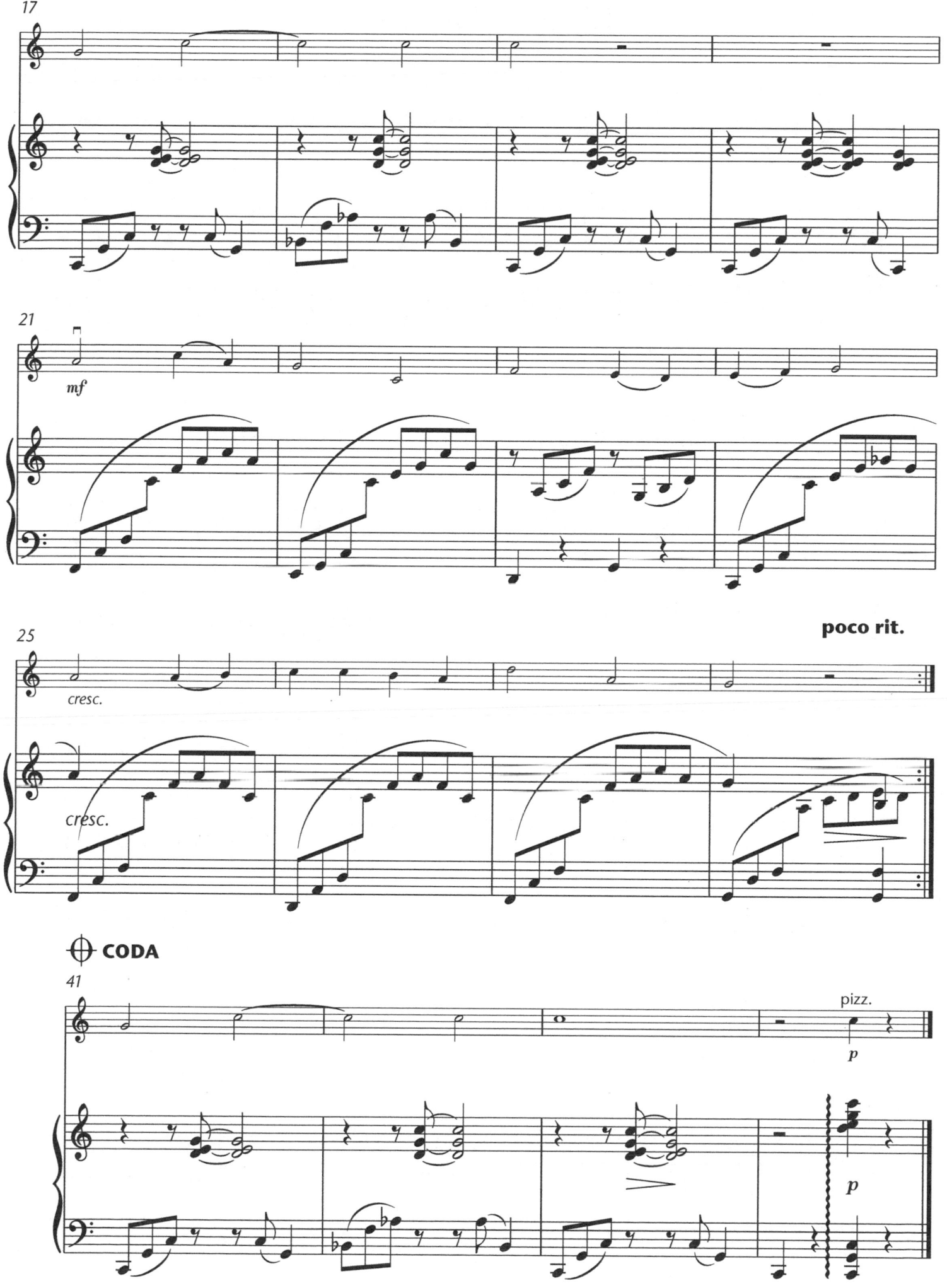

2

# 18. Yodelling song

German folk tune

# 20. Romani band

KB & DB

# 21. Ten thousand miles away

Sea shanty

**With a good swing**

# 22. I got those fiddle blues

KB & DB

# 23. Air in G

J. C. Bach

# 24. Prelude from 'Te Deum'

Charpentier

# 25. That's how it goes!

KB & DB

# 26. Hari coo coo

Indian lullaby

# 27. Summer evening

KB & DB

# 28. Flamenco dance

KB & DB

# 29. Adam in the garden

Jamaican folk tune

# 30. Somebody's knocking at your door

Spiritual

# 31. The old chariot

Sea shanty

# 32. Air

Handel

# 34. Winter song

KB & DB

Nos. 33 and 34 are reversed to avoid a page turn.

# 33. The wee cooper o' Fife

Scottish folk tune

# 35. Rory O'More

Traditional Irish Jig

# 37. Aerobics!

KB & DB

Nos. 36 and 37 are reversed to avoid a page turn.

# 36. Trick cyclist

KB & DB

**With energy**

# 38. Caribbean sunshine

KB & DB